RSAC

D0801447

NOV 2007

bow the

UNIVERSE

First published in the United States of America in 2004

by **UNIVERSE PUBLISHING**

A Division of Rizzoli International Publications, Inc.

300 Park Avenue South

New York, NY 10010

www.rizzoliusa.com

© 2004 artlist INTERNATIONAL

TEXT BY: Tricia Levi

DESIGN BY: Lisa Vaughn-Soraghan, Two of Cups Design

ADDITIONAL DESIGN BY: Sara E. Stemen

2005   2006   2007   2008   /   10   9   8   7   6   5   4   3   2

Printed in China

ISBN: 0-7893-1190-9

LIBRARY OF CONGRESS CATALOG CONTROL NUMBER: 2004104734

contents

Akita **8**

American Pit Bull Terrier **12**

Basset Hound **16**

Beagle **20**

Bernese Mountain Dog **24**

Bloodhound **28**

Border Collie **32**

Boston Terrier **36**

Boxer **40**

Brussels Griffon **44**

Bulldog **48**

Bull Terrier **52**

Cavalier King Charles Spaniel **56**

Chihuahua **60**

Chinese Shar-pei **64**

Chow Chow **68**

Cocker Spaniel **72**

Collie **76**

Dachshund **80**

Dalmatian **84**

Dandie Dinmont Terrier **88**

Doberman Pinscher **92**

English Cocker Spaniel **96**

French Bulldog **100**

German Shepherd **104**
Golden Retriever **108**
Great Pyrenees **112**

Irish Setter **116**
Italian Greyhound **120**

Jack Russell Terrier **124**
Japanese Terrier **128**

Labrador Retriever **132**
Lakeland Terrier **136**

Maltese **140**
Manchester Terrier **144**
Miniature Pinscher **148**
Miniature Schnauzer **152**

Norfolk & Norwich Terrier **156**

Papillon **160**
Pekingese **164**

Pembroke Welsh Corgi **168**

Pomeranian **172**

Poodle **176**

Pug **180**

Rottweiler **184**

Tibetan Spaniel **208**

Weimaraner **212**

West Highland White Terrier **216**

Yorkshire Terrier **220**

Dog Groups Defined **224**

Saluki **188**

Scottish Terrier **192**

Shetland Sheepdog **196**

Shih Tzu **200**

Siberian Husky **204**

akita

good luck charm

Considered a symbol of health, happiness, and a long life in Japan, this hunting dog of very large quarry—from deer to black bears!—was and still is considered a national treasure in its native country. Though the breed has existed for hundreds of years and was a favorite of Japanese nobility, it has been popular in the United States only since World War II, when soldiers brought the curly tailed, upright-eared dogs home. Big, powerful, vigilant, and extremely loyal, Akitas make excellent guards.

dog dish:

Belongs to Working Group

Originated in Japan

Agile and alert

24 to 28 inches tall

american
pit bull
terrier

much
misunderstood

Looks can be deceiving. With a somewhat forbidding appearance due to a distinctive large head, muscular body, far-apart
eyes, pointy upright ears, and confident "tough guy" gait, this
actually is a friendly, eager-to-please breed. Aggressiveness
toward people is unusual and toward other dogs can be con-
strained with proper training and socialization. American pit
bulls are highly intelligent dogs that combine the bravery of
terriers and the strength of bulldogs.

american pit bull terrier

basset hound

| bow the dog

laid-back & low-key

Utterly irresistible is this sweet, gentle breed of extremes with short, wrinkly skinned legs punctuated by extra-large paws; lengthy bodies; long, droopy ears; a sad-eyed expression; and a slow and plodding, though not clumsy, bearing. Normally easygoing and unflappable, basset hounds make it known when they catch a scent (only bloodhounds have a better sense of smell) at which time their musical hound voices are heard loud and clear. They are independent-minded but make devoted companions.

dog dish:

Belongs to Hound Group

Originated in France

Steady and serene

14 inches tall

basset hound

beagle

dog dish:

Belongs to Hound Group

Originated in England

Spunky and sociable

Under 15 inches tall

favorite
faithful friend

One of the all-time most popular breeds is this smallest of the scent hounds. Happy, outgoing dogs with good hound voices, beagles make excellent companions who enjoy being with people and get along with other pets. Their soft, brown eyes have a sweet, pleading expression that can melt the hardest of hearts. Cleverness, curiosity, and quickness—essential when they were rabbit hunters in England—are still important characteristics. They are high-energy little dogs and need a lot of exercise to stay fit and happy.

bernese
mountain dog

supersize and sturdy

Talk about a whole lotta dog! An ancient breed whose forebears were brought into Switzerland 2,000 years ago by invading Romans, these huge, hardy dogs were used to pull heavy loads and drive cattle, and as watchdogs on farms. Though their natural way of moving is slow and measured—who's going to rush them?—these congenial, good-natured dogs can pick up the pace when necessary. They require only moderate amounts of exercise, making them excellent house and apartment pets.

dog dish:

Belongs to Working Group

🐾

Originated in Switzerland

🐾

Sweet and sometimes shy

🐾

23 to 27 inches tall

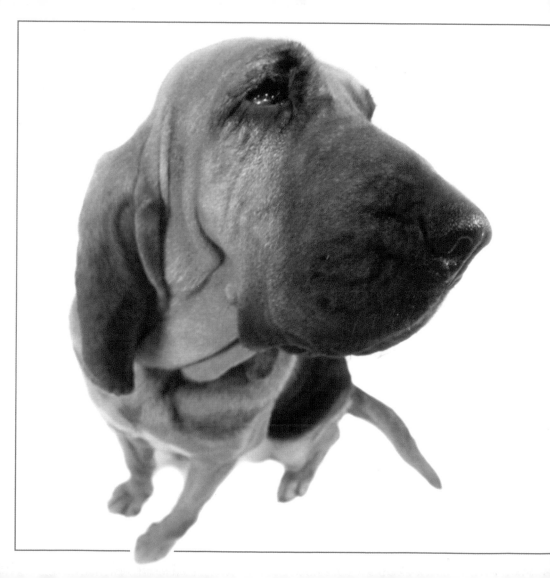

blood-
hound

| bow the dog

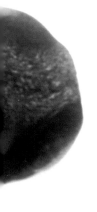

serious scent-smeller

Looking like the wise elder statesman of the canine world with its characteristic wrinkly, loose skin around its head and neck, this solemn-faced dog often has an important job to do—locating missing people. Incomparable senses of smell and determined dispositions allow blood-hounds to follow trails—

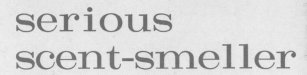

even those that are cold—over hundreds of miles. Though large powerhouses, they can be somewhat shy; however, they are affectionate and gentle with people and other animals and are not aggressive.

bloodhound

border collie

dog dish:

Belongs to Herding Group

Originated in
Scotland and England

Spry and spirited

18 to 22 inches tall

speedy
sheepherder

Extremely intelligent, swift,
and graceful, this work lover
requires these traits to do
the job it was bred for:
corralling the woolly ones.
Border collies have been relied
on for hundreds of years to do
just that task. An ability to focus
intensely and an eagerness to
please enable them to excel at
their jobs. They like to be
active, so owners (preferably
those with energy to spare)
need to keep these enjoyable
family companions occupied.

boston
terrier

| bow the dog

tuxedo-clad gentleman

One of the few native breeds of the United States, this dignified little dog is nicknamed American Gentleman. A cross between two fighters—an English bulldog and kind of English terrier—today these lively dogs have gentle temperaments. This is a far cry from their combative past. Expressive soft, dark eyes reveal their intelligence and kindness. Attention is relished, and they make loving companions for both city and country people.

dog dish:

Belongs to Non-Sporting Group

Originated in America

Congenial and cheery

Ranges from under 15 up to 25 pounds

boxer

proud, playful pooch

Fun-loving and jolly is this bulldog-related breed, originally used in the savage sports of bullbaiting and dogfighting. Affable and intelligent, today boxers often put their smarts to work in police training. When they're not on the job, these dignified dogs—with distinctive black masks and expressive faces—make happy family companions, exhibiting particular patience with children. Their natural exuberance needs to be reined in a bit with a firm hand, but they are highly trainable. Short muzzles and coats make them unable to tolerate very hot or cold temperatures.

dog dish:

Belongs to Working Group

Originated in Germany

Friendly and fun-loving

21 to 25 inches tall

brussels
griffon

dog dish:

Belongs to Toy Group

Originated in Belgium

Sensitive and smart

8 to 10 pounds

pretty on
the inside

Slightly odd-looking with very prominent black eyes
and lengthy lashes, a flat nose set
between the eyes, a prominent
chin, and lots of wiry facial hair,
this dog makes up for its unusual
visage with a big, exuberant
personality and an almost
humanlike expression.
Several centuries old,
this toy breed has a
not-so-regal lineage—
a mix of German affen-
pinscher and Belgian
street terrier. Brussels
griffons are vivacious
little packages of good-
natured fun.

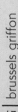

brussels griffon

bulldog

happy-go-lucky one

This jowly, wrinkly faced friend was originally a fighter involved in bullbaiting, a sport in which fearlessness and ferocity were required. Today bulldogs are serene and stately. Low-to-the-ground wide loads who look like bruisers, they actually can be delicate flowers who wilt in the hot weather (due to their short muzzles); a cool room indoors is key. Their unusual gait, a sideways shuffle, is specific to their breed. Easygoing family pets, bulldogs do not require much exercise.

bull
terrier

once a warrior, now a sweetie

An egg-shaped head and triangular, very dark eyes are distinctive features of this spirited, happy dog who once had the unpleasant job of baiting bulls. Descended from two fighting breeds—the bulldog and the extinct English terrier—bull terriers had to be brave, strong, and very fast to achieve this task. Today, the fight has been bred out of them, and they are sweet and affectionate, making loving and loyal friends.

cavalier
king charles
spaniel

bow the dog

perky pooch of privilege

Large, dark eyes and floppy, long-haired ears give these dogs of royalty kindly countenances, which are matched by their outgoing demeanors. Active and easy to train, these intelligent toy spaniels were favorites of England's King Charles II in the seventeenth century and are still popular in that country today. They have lovely silky, moderately long locks and are diminutive enough in size that they can live in small spaces. Exercise is key for this breed.

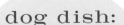

dog dish:

Belongs to Toy Group

Originated in England

Gentle and graceful

12 to 13 inches tall

cavalier king charles spaniel

59

chihuahua

| bow the dog

dog dish:

Belongs to Toy Group

Originated in Mexico

Delightful and deft

Under 6 pounds

teensy-weensy tyke

Confidence is not in short supply with this tiny one, an ancient breed of native Central Americans. Chihuahuas have unique head shapes with rounded skulls and ears that flare out to the side when at rest. Though minute in size, they are courageous watchdogs who will defend their territory; they are not friendly with other dogs. Because they are so small and have delicate constitutions, they are primarily indoor pets—especially when it is cold outside.

chinese
shar-pei

emperor's pet

This breed has existed in China since 200 B.C. and was first brought to the United States in the mid '60s to save it: These dogs were nearly wiped out, purposefully, during China's Communist revolution. An abundance of loose skin and wrinkles around the face and body and deep-set eyes, front-flopping ears, and a scowling expression give this dog its one-of-a-kind somber countenance. Like one of its compatriots, the chow chow, this dog has a blue-black or lavender tongue. It is independent-minded but devoted.

dog dish:

Belongs to Non-Sporting Group

Originated in China

Intelligent and intense

18 to 20 inches tall

chow
chow

little lion
look-alike

An ancient Chinese breed that dates back 2,000 years,
this working dog excelled at hunting, herding, hauling,
and guarding. Aloof, independent, and most definitely
haughty—just look at that frown—is this bushy-coated,
curly tailed, stout and sturdy dog with the characteristic
mane of hair around its face. Chow grooming is a major
undertaking: the coat requires twice-weekly brushing.
Like shar-peis, chows' deep-set eyes limit peripheral
vision—something to keep in mind when approaching
these dogs.

dog dish:

Belongs to Non-Sporting Group

🐾

Originated in China

🐾

Sturdy and serious

🐾

17 to 20 inches tall

chow chow

cocker spaniel

Belongs to Sporting Group

🐾

Originated in England

🐾

Devoted and demonstrative

🐾

14 to 15 inches tall

best buddy

One of the favorite breeds in the United States—and the world's most popular spaniel—is this cheerful, good-natured dog. Relatively low to the ground, it was once known to drive woodcocks out from cover or out of the water. A soft coat of silky straight or wavy hair; long, floppy, hair-covered ears; and soft, round eyes give this dog its sweet look. Playful, intelligent, and easy to train, cockers make wonderfully huggable companions for either country or city people. They are supremely affectionate and form lasting attachments to their owners.

cocker spaniel

collie

sophisticated scot

In the atypical position of being both working dogs for shepherds and friends to royalty—Queen Victoria was a huge fan—is this venerable breed from Scotland. Although collies are highly adaptable to city or country life, they require plenty of exercise to be happy; after all, they were bred for herding cows and sheep to market. They love to protect—people, especially children, as well as property. Collies can have short-haired coats, but when most people think of these lovely dogs, the long-haired Lassie immediately comes to mind.

dog dish:

Belongs to Herding Group

Originated in Scotland

Smart and strong

22 to 26 inches tall

dachshund

dog dish:

Belongs to Hound Group

Originated in Germany

Curious and confident

Ranges from under 11
up to 32 pounds

not your average frankfurter

Cheerful and active are these little long-backed guys, nicknamed hot dogs, who scamper along the street—with tiny legs in overdrive—trying to keep up with their owners. *Dachshund* is German for "badger dog," and the breed's original job was to hunt that prey, as well as other small game. Shiny, dark eyes with a sweet, alert expression and floppy ears are cute features of these affectionate and playful pets who can adapt to both the city and the country. Odor-free coats come in short- , wire- , and long-haired varieties.

dalmatian

dotted dog

Black or occasionally brown are the spots that distinguish this breed, making it instantly identifiable. In the past, dalmatians were jacks-of-all-trades: masters of herding sheep, pulling cars, and tracking and retrieving game. They also had an affinity for horses, so they were used to clear the paths for fire carriages. These devoted, loving dogs are high-energy and need to be active. Puppies are solid white, and develop their dime- to half-dollar-sized spots when they are bigger.

dandie dinmont terrier

dog dish:

Belongs to Terrier Group
🐾
Originated in England and Scotland
🐾
Intelligent and independent
🐾
8 to 11 inches tall

little canine that can

A dignified, tenacious dynamo is this long and low dog, with a distinctive white fluffy puff at the top of its head. This breed was especially adept at catching otters and badgers in the past. Clowning around comes naturally to the active Dandie Dinmonts, independent-minded pepper- or mustard-colored terriers, who love children and act as excellent protectors. They are wonderful family dogs that enjoy city or country life but can be a bit reserved with strangers.

dandie dinmont terrier

doberman
pinscher

creative combo

A German dog first bred in the late 1800s, it is a mix of many: Rottweiler, German pinscher (*pinscher* means "terrier" in German), black and tan terrier, and other dogs. As workers, Dobermans have been trained to do jobs such as guarding military troops and police, finding criminals, and guiding the blind. They are excellent family companions, too. Sleek, with sharp features and shiny coats, are these determined and intelligent dogs, who require patient and consistent training to be their best.

dog dish:

Belongs to Working Group

Originated in Germany

Powerful and proud

24 to 28 inches tall

english cocker spaniel

sweet-eyed sidekick

Looking like the somewhat taller and heavier cousin of the cocker spaniel is this venerable breed, a hunter's companion and helper that once flushed out and retrieved game. Special features of English cockers are long, dangly ears and dark, expressive eyes. These cheerful, affectionate dogs have a gentle countenance and a lovely abundance of silky-soft hair. Able to make themselves at home in apartments or houses, they, like cocker spaniels, enjoy nothing better than being beside their adored owners.

dog dish:

Belongs to Sporting Group

Originated in England

Sensitive and sunny

15 to 17 inches tall

french
bulldog

love moi!

Sprightly and sweet-natured is this wonderful companion who basks in attention, is especially friendly with children, *and* gets along with other animals to boot! The faces of French bulldogs have character in spades: short muzzles; wrinkled foreheads; black noses; round, dark eyes; and unique bat ears. Broad chests, squat and muscular wrestler-type bodies, and wide-apart, pudgy legs distinguish these French favorites— English and toy bulldog mixes—that rarely bark. They have short and shiny easy-care coats and can adapt to life in small apartments or houses.

dog dish:

Belongs to Non-Sporting Group

🐾

Originated in France

🐾

Smart and steady

🐾

Under 28 pounds

german
shepherd

cool as a cucumber

Incomparable composure and confidence, along with keen intelligence, are why more of these dogs than any other are used for search-and-rescue, tracking, seeing-eye, police, and military work. As family pets, they are loving friends who enjoy attention and are game for adventure. Their harsh, medium-length outer coats—characteristic colors being tan with a distinctive black muzzle and saddle—shed year-round and need frequent brushing. Calm demeanors make them approachable, yet they can be reserved and do not make fast friends of strangers.

dog dish:

Belongs to Herding Group

Originated in Germany

Noble and nimble

22 to 26 inches tall

golden retriever

Belongs to Sporting Group

Originated in Scotland

Strong and sporty

21 to 24 inches tall

popular pal

One of the favorite breeds in the United States, these medium-sized, lovable, huggable, drop-eared dogs make excellent and good-natured pets who readily befriend people and animals. Early varieties were mixes of yellow English retrievers and water spaniels. It was important to develop dogs that were amenable to being wet and cold because they were needed to collect fowl on land and in water when on the hunt. This eager and athletic breed fit the bill, helped by a dense and water-repellent golden-colored double coat. Though these outgoing dogs are adaptable to both apartment and house life, they require daily exercise.

great
pyrenees

dog dish:

Belongs to Working Group
👣
Originated in Central Asia
or Siberia
👣
Keen and kind
👣
25 to 32 inches tall

impressive defender

Massive and muscular is this breed, which for thousands of years had the responsibility of protecting sheep from predators in the mountains. Intrepid and imposing, Great Pyreneeses faced down wolves and bears that wanted to feast on their flocks. Their thick, mostly white coats—which sometimes have markings of gray, reddish brown, or tan—are water resistant. This enables the dogs to survive extreme weather conditions. Hefty protectors, they weigh in at a substantial 85 to 100 pounds but are gentle with their families. Firmness is required to keep these strong-willed dogs from taking over, though.

irish setter

redheaded beauty

The most distinctive feature of this agile hunter—one of the largest of the sporting breeds—is its mahogany or chestnut-red coat. Flat, glossy, and of moderate length, its hair requires a bit of care: a good brushing every week. Adult Irish setters have lovely feathered and fringed hair on their ears, bodies, and legs. Vivacious and active, these dogs love to play and have fun, and they require plenty of regular exercise. With a graceful stride when walking or trotting—and long, slender head held high—this breed's aristocratic character is readily apparent.

dog dish:

Belongs to Sporting Group

🐾

Originated in Ireland

🐾

Amiable and animated

🐾

25 to 27 inches tall

italian
greyhound

bow the dog

your lap, please!

Originating more than 2,000 years ago in the Mediterranean and a favorite of royalty and the upper classes, it is possible that this greyhound-related breed was one of the first to be specifically developed as a companion pet. Everything about this diminutive lapdog is slender and elegant, from the head to the neck, body, and legs.

Italian greyhounds barely shed, require little grooming, and always smell as fresh as a daisy (or at least are odor free!). Though they need to wear sweaters in cold weather, these dogs, with adorable ears and high-stepping strides, are hardy and enjoy frolicking in the fresh air.

italian greyhound

jack russell
terrier

great ball of feistiness

Spryness, intelligence, and determination are important characteristics of this breed and have been since the days when Jack Russells were fox hunters in England. Thanks to compact, flexible chests, they had the ability to pursue quarry both above and below ground. Their relentlessness and bravery—essential on the hunt—continue to be pronounced traits, as are their high-spirited and exceptionally affectionate natures. Athletic and energetic, these dogs require regular exercise to stay fit and happy.

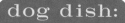

japanese
terrier

dog dish:

Belongs to Terrier Group

🐾

Originated in Japan

🐾

Affectionate and affable

🐾

About 12 inches tall

tri-toned and toy-sized

Developed in the eighteenth century by mixing imported smooth fox and local terriers is this happy, playful, and slender-legged breed. Petite in stature, Japanese terriers were created to be companions who could be carried along when their owners went out. Their smooth, sleek coats—darker colored on the head and lighter colored on the body, sometimes with black markings—are easy to groom, and their upright, side-flared ears and oval-shaped eyes give them a sweet countenance. Like their terrier relatives, these dogs are lively and alert. They are fun pets who enjoy romping around in the fresh air, but the breed is rare outside of Japan.

labrador
retriever

loyal
for life

Extreme intelligence, the ability to learn quickly, and an unflappable temperament are qualities that enable this breed to successfully accomplish seeing-eye and search-and-rescue work. Originally fishermen's helpers with the job of pulling in nets and catching stray fish, Labs later were crossed with setters, spaniels, and other retrievers to develop today's breed. Wonderful family dogs, they are friendly and nonaggressive toward people and other animals. A short, straight, weather-resistant coat, which comes in black, yellow, or chocolate; cute drop ears; and kind eyes complete this lovable dog package.

labrador retriever

lakeland terrier

let's go, let's go, let's go!

Always ready for action is this courageous, confident fox hunter, one of the oldest working terrier breeds still in existence. Joie de vivre and boundless energy for fun and games make Lakeland terriers excellent pets. Unique features include sturdy, narrow bodies (thinness enabled them to squeeze into rocky fox dens) and weather-resistant double coats with hard, wiry outer layers and soft under layers. Coat colors include blue or black marked with tan, bluish black, grizzle, red, or wheaten; a black saddle can be present as well. A long-hair-topped muzzle and a rectangular-shaped face also distinguish this playful pooch.

lakeland terrier

dog dish:

Belongs to Toy Group

Originated in Italy

Spunky and sprightly

4 to 6 pounds

mediterranean munchkin

Snow white hair—and lots of it!—is what stands out when this tiny dog glides by. Those abundant tresses are fine and silky and cover the entire body and flipped-over-the-back tail. Daily brushing and frequent washing are essential to maintain the locks of this venerable breed, which has existed for thousands of years, looking luxurious. Mini-mites sizewise but blithe and brave in disposition, they aren't pushovers, that's for sure. They are devoted and fun family pets.

manchester terrier

petite perfection

Compact and well-proportioned, this breed—a mix of the black-and-tan terrier with whippet and greyhound—is elegance personified. The jet black-with-mahogany coat is short, shiny, and sleek, and its bright eyes convey attentiveness and intelligence. The two varieties, standard and toy, are identical in all ways except size and ear shape; they have the same distinctive tan markings. Energetic and active, both types make fun family pets who are devoted and loyal, although sometimes they are reserved with strangers.

dog dish:

Belongs to Terrier Group

🐾

Originated in England

🐾

Athletic and agile

🐾

12 to 22 pounds (standard);
Under 12 pounds (toy)

miniature pinscher

tiny bundle
of fun!

Self-possessed and peppy is this little dog
with an outsized, headstrong personality.
Not related to Dobermans, but possibly a
mix of German pinscher, dachshund, and
Italian greyhound, this dog is vivacious
and fearless. Min-pins love to frolic and
enjoy being both indoors and out,
but only moderate exercise is
necessary. Their tight,
sleek, and easy-
care coats—
which come in red,
stag red (with some
black hairs), black and
tan, and chocolate—require
practically no attention.
Affectionate and devoted,
they develop close attachments
to their owners.

dog dish:

Belongs to Toy Group

🐾

Originated in Germany

🐾

High-stepping and high-energy

🐾

10 to 12½ inches tall

miniature schnauzer

dog dish:

Belongs to Terrier Group
🐾
Originated in Germany
🐾
Friendly and feisty
🐾
12 to 14 inches tall

distinctly dignified

Bushy eyebrows and a thick beard and mustache create this breed's sagelike visage. (One feels these dogs should be suited up in wool jackets with elbow patches.) But that's just their outward appearance! At heart, these rectangular-headed dogs are youthful, enjoying play and fun; after all, they are members of the always-lively terrier clan. One of three schnauzer breeds—standard, giant, and miniature—developed in Germany, this variety is a mix of standard schnauzer, affenpinscher, and poodle. Happy and hardy, these dogs were originally farm workers who caught pests; today they are primarily house pets.

miniature schnauzer

norfolk &
norwich
terrier

dog dish:

Belongs to Terrier Group

🐾

Originated in England

🐾

Active and agile

🐾

Under 10 inches tall

spunk
squared

Spirited and spry are the terrier twins: the drop-eared
Norfolk and the prick-eared Norwich. Until the mid
'60s, these two varieties were
considered the same breed.
Sparkling dark, oval-shaped eyes
convey their keen intelligence,
which was required in the past
when they were hunting for foxes and
other farmyard pests. Both breeds are
hardy with wiry, weather-resistant
coats that come in a variety of colors
including shades of red, wheaten, and
black and tan. They have boundless
energy, revel in playtime, and make
amusing, affectionate family pets.

norfolk & norwich terrier

papillon

the french butterfly

Prominent on these dainty dogs are their well-feathered butterfly-shaped ears (*papillon* means "butterfly" in French). Long, straight tresses are another important feature and, as on the ears, hair is profuse on the chest and the curled-over-the-back tail. Don't let the diminutive dimensions of papillons fool you, though. While comely and delicate-looking, these lapdogs are also lively and robust, enjoying outdoors play in hot or cold weather. They make excellent, devoted pets for city and country dwellers, and they like nothing more than being beside their beloved owners.

peKingese

dog dish:

Belongs to Toy Group

Originated in China

Self-confident and stately

Under 14 pounds

all about
attitude!

Renowned for being independent and intractable is this dignified, millennia-enduring breed. No coddling or warm laps are necessary for this headstrong dog—and owners wouldn't have it any other way! Entertaining and enjoyable, Pekingese like to run around and play and are fearless in the face of danger. With flat frontal features surrounded by massive manes, copious coats, and plush tails carried proudly over the back, these dogs have a unique appearance. Considered sacred in ancient China, they were reserved for members of the royal family only (stealing the dogs incurred the ultimate punishment).

pekingese

pembroke welsh corgi

queen's companion

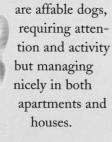

Short-legged and long-backed with upright ears and a foxlike head is this "dwarf dog" (*corgi* in Welsh), the favorite breed of England's Queen Elizabeth II. Originally a cattle dog, this sweet-faced low-to-the-grounder has a strong build and a soft, thick double coat that sheds year-round; the outer coat is weather resistant. Lively and enthusiastic, corgis are affable dogs, requiring attention and activity but managing nicely in both apartments and houses.

dog dish:

Belongs to Herding Group

🐾

Originated in Wales

🐾

Companionable and kind

🐾

10 to 12 inches tall

pomeranian

fluffy ball o' fur

Surprisingly, this wee one is descended from the heavy-duty sled dogs of Iceland and Lapland. Pomeranians were bred down and down and down in size to the featherweight (in poundage only!) breed of today. Very lively and outgoing, with bright eyes and an alert and foxlike expression, they make amusing family pets and, though they may look fragile, are no pushovers. Unique features include luxurious manes of hair; itty-bitty upright ears; tiny, dark eyes and noses; extra-thick double coats, with the top hairs standing on end; and feathery, fanned-over-the-back tails.

Belongs to Toy Group

Originated in Iceland

Independent and inquisitive

3 to 7 pounds

poodle

dog dish:

Non-Sporting and Toy Group

Originated in Germany

Proud and powerful

Under 10 inches tall (toy);
10 to 15 inches tall (miniature);
over 15 inches tall
(standard)

canine of the froufrou 'do

Often seen with the fancy-pants hairstyle, though lovely looking with a more casual cut, is this breed with the unusual curly coat that makes it immediately identifiable. (Curls become cords if hair is not properly maintained.) Models of dignity, poodles stride along in a confident, head-held-high style. By the mid '50s, the qualities that made them excellent pets—intelligence, calmness, trainability, and devotion to family—catapulted them into top-dog status. This was the number-one breed for nearly twenty years! The three poodle types—standard, miniature, and toy—are all considered one breed, the only difference being size.

poodle

pug

those eyes . . .
that mug!

Bulging dark eyes and a prominent wrinkly face (as well as a curly tail) are unique features of this easy-to-adore breed, one of the oldest in existence. Pugs are solid though small soft-coated dogs and have existed since 400 B.C., when they were the companions of Buddhist monks in Tibet. Amiable and affectionate, they make great pets and are especially kid-friendly. They easily adapt to city or country life and are charmers known for their senses of humor and love of games.

dog dish:

Belongs to Toy Group

🐾

Originated in China

🐾

Amusing and affable

🐾

14 to 18 pounds

rottweiler

dog dish:

Belongs to Working Group

🐾

Originated in Germany
(modern Rottweiler)

🐾

Self-possessed and steady

🐾

22 to 27 inches tall

teutonic titan

Massive, muscular, yet mild-mannered is this German breed with its characteristic glossy black coat and rust markings. Named after the town in which it was bred, Rottweil, this dog spent its early days as a cattle driver and guard. Today, exercise is essential, and any outdoor adventure is welcome. Early and firm obedience training of Rottweilers, which their size and strength demand, can rein in aggressiveness. Keen protective instincts and a sense of loyalty make them constant compan-ions—literally: They never want to lose sight of their owners and will follow them around the house.

rottweiler

saluki

| bow the dog

Belongs to Hound Group

Originated in Africa

Dignified and devoted

23 to 28 inches tall (females
are much smaller)

gazellelike grace

Like prey, like predator. Built for speed, with slender bodies and long legs, these esteemed dogs of ancient Egyptian royalty also used excellent eyesight and endurance to successfully hunt gazelle. Today, getting lots of activity, though of a more playful nature, is required. They are related to large hounds, such as the Afghan, borzoi, greyhound, and Irish wolfhound, and are possibly the oldest domesticated dogs in existence (they were mummified when they died, like their pharaoh friends). A short coat with silky clusters of long hair on the ears, legs, and tail gives this proud and powerful dog a unique look.

saluki

scottish terrier

mature
manner

Character-packed is one way to describe the overall effect of this distinguished diminutive dog's facial features. Hairy beards, mustaches, and bushy brows adorning rectangular-shaped heads, in addition to penetrating expressions and pricked ears, make Scottish terriers look downright professorial. This appearance belies their spryness—they delight in romping around and rollicking. Playful as puppies, they can become more solemn and sedate as adults—but not stodgy! They are devoted companions to their human friends.

Belongs to Terrier Group

Originated in Scotland

Sturdy and spirited

10 inches tall

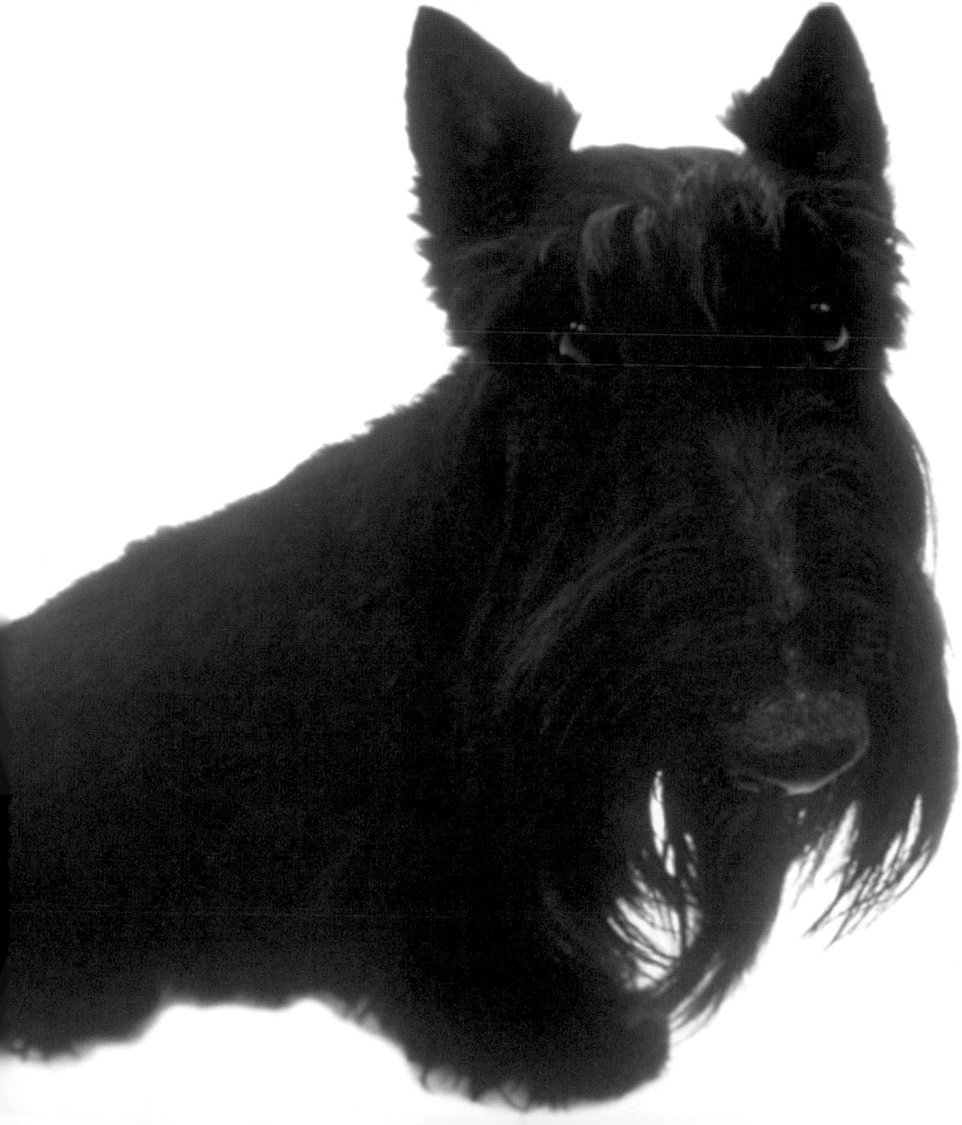

shetland
sheepdog

collie cousin

Looking like the twin of the long-haired collie is this smaller, plusher breed developed on the Shetland Islands, off the coast of Scotland. Exceptionally intelligent, sweet, and gentle is this beautiful dog, whose forebear is the border collie and whose purpose was to watch over herds of sheep. Abundant, thick straight hair that stands on end is the Shetland sheepdog's most readily apparent feature. Compact, this dog doesn't need a lot of room to move, so fares well in both city and country environments. Shetlands form close bonds with their owners.

dog dish:

Belongs to Herding Group

🐾

Originated in
Shetland Islands, Scotland

🐾

Quick and clever

🐾

13 to 16 inches tall

shih tzu

dog dish:

Belongs to Toy Group

🐾

Originated in Tibet

🐾

Smart and spry

🐾

8 to 11 inches

tibetan
fluffy pup

Lush locks, a beard and mustache, a short
and hairy muzzle, and a feathery tail
transported over the back are distin-
guishing characteristics of this ancient
Tibetan breed, developed in China. Shih tzu
are sturdy little dogs, crosses of the Lhasa
apso or Tibetan mountain dog and the
Pekingese, that move smoothly with a
proud, head-held-high carriage, a vestige of
their heritage as the favorite companions
of Chinese royals. Sprightly and spunky
with a distinct stubborn streak are these
sociable, fun-loving little ones. They are
affectionate and friendly with everyone,
including strangers and other animals.

shih tzu

siberian husky

stamina
in spades

Developed in Siberia by the Chukchi tribe, this breed was
used to haul sleds and herd reindeer across vast distances in
ice-cold temperatures. Strong and compact with thick double
coats and confident, can-do attitudes, these agreeable dogs
were—and are still—always ready to go. Today, their work
includes pulling sleds in races, which is done efficiently thanks
in part to large feet with hair between the toes (hair allows the
dogs to grip the ice). Those bright eyes, which can be blue or
brown (or one of each!), and upright ears reveal their keen
intelligence and alertness. They come in a variety of colors but
typically have a white foreface and belly.

dog dish:

Belongs to Working Group
🐾
Originated in Siberia
🐾
Gentle and graceful
🐾
20 to 23½ inches tall

tibetan
spaniel

wee watchdog

An ancient breed that was prized in Tibet and was often given as a gift to Chinese nobility, this small-faced dog with a fluffy, plumelike tail and feathery ears has sentry (not lap) duty in his blood: He sat on high walls at monasteries watching for intruders with his keen eyesight. Today, Tibetan spaniels love play, not pampering. Expressive-eyed with affable, affectionate, and active dispositions, they make excellent family companions. Other animals, including dogs, can become fast friends; that's not the case with strangers.

tibetan spaniel

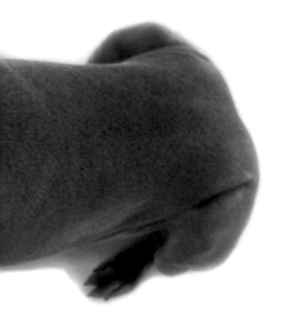

weimaraner

Belongs to Sporting Group

🐾

Originated in Germany

🐾

Intelligent and intrepid

🐾

23 to 27 inches tall

silver streak

Newbies, comparatively, these beautiful large, gray dogs were first developed in the 1800s to hunt big game—bears, mountain lions, and wolves—and were intended exclusively for the blue-blood set. This bloodhound-related breed with piercing light-colored eyes and a good sense of smell is strong and sleek with serious stamina. Weimaraners have dominating dispositions that demand a firm and confident hand in training; otherwise, they will soon rule the roost. Plenty of exercise is also essential. They are loving family members who require attention and human friendship in order to be happy.

west highland
white
terrier

jolly and joyful

Perpetually cheerful with its tail often wagging in anticipation of meeting and greeting new friends is this spunky dog. All-white little terriers, with sweet round faces, Westies are very active and surprisingly fast. They were bred to be speedy, as their early days were spent sniffing out and hunting down unwanted farmyard pests. Inherent inquisitiveness and intelligence are revealed in their expressions. Great companions, they are affectionate, playful, and friendly. Westies's impishness is a favorite characteristic of these beloved pets.

yorkshire
terrier

don't mess with me!

These dogs may be tiny, but they're not timid. Natives of England, these were working dogs before becoming the pampered house pets of the upper crust in the late nineteenth century. They carry themselves with confidence and, as with other terriers, they're curious and independent. Their sparkling eyes reveal their keen intelligence. Pretty-as-a-picture adults have a lot of hair. It is floor length and straight and a bow tie or two up top keeps the hair out of their eyes.

dog dish:

Belongs to Toy Group

🐾

Originated in England

🐾

Inquisitive and independent

🐾

About 7 pounds

yorkshire terrier

dog groups defined

HERDING DOGS

Breeds in this group have been helpmates to farmers and shepherds for hundreds of years. Their job: herding sheep and cattle. Corralling comes naturally for the members of this group—they do it even without training. The desire to herd is so strong that they'll attempt to gather any animals—or people—if the opportunity arises. Because they were bred to run around keeping their charges in check, these active and intelligent dogs require plenty of exercise.

HOUNDS

Breeds in this group were developed as hunters' helpers. Their role: to scout for and track prey. They are divided into two categories: scent hounds, which hunt using their exceptional senses of smell, and sighthounds, which hunt using their keen eyesight. These dogs are very affectionate and aim to please.

NON-SPORTING DOGS

Breeds in this catchall category range in size and personality. They are in this group because they don't completely fit into any other category and some have long since stopped doing the work for which they were originally bred. These dogs make wonderful companions.

SPORTING DOGS

Helping bird hunters is what the breeds in this group were developed to do. Each kind of breed had a specific task: the retriever collected birds and other game shot by hunters; the setter found the game and froze in front of it; and the spaniel scared game birds out of their hiding places. As a group, these dogs are all-around excellent companions—they were bred to be—and need plenty of exercise.

TERRIERS

Dogs in this group are feisty and fearless, no matter what their size. They needed to be brave to do the job they were bred for—hunting vermin. They became excellent diggers—and dig they will do to this day if they catch the right scent. These dogs are strong-willed, which makes them challenging to train, but the hard work pays off.

TOY DOGS

Big personalities in tiny packages is one way to describe the members of this group—the smallest dogs bred. Companions, they are used to sitting on laps and being carried around. They are very gentle and love attention. Special care needs to be taken with them because of their size: they must be handled carefully and can't tolerate temperature extremes. Living in small spaces is fine for these little ones.

WORKING DOGS

These dogs were bred to help with a variety of tasks such as hauling loads and protecting farm animals. Often having heavy-duty jobs to perform, many of these dogs are very large and strong. Training these independent thinkers is important—both for socialization and control purposes. They can be protective, a trait that was required when they were guards and watchdogs. They may be oversize but they often have gentle dispositions.